A Challenge to Chu

A Table For All

Inderjit Bhogal

President
British Methodist Conference
2000 - 2001

Penistone Publications

First Published in Great Britain in 2000 by Penistone Publications

© 2000 Inderjit Singh Bhogal

The moral right of Inderjit Singh Bhogal to be identified as the author of this work has been asserted in accordance with the Copyright, Designs and Patents Act of 1988.

All rights reserved. No part of this publication may be reproduced, stored in a retrieval system, or transmitted in any form or by any means, electronic, mechanical, photocopying, recording, or otherwise, without the prior permission of both the copyright owner and the above publisher of this book.

ISBN: 0 9538793 0 5

Printed in Great Britain by
John Brailsford Print
Rotherham, South Yorkshire

Published by:
Penistone Publications
61 Talbot Road, Penistone,
Sheffield, South Yorkshire, S36 9ED

Introduction

My vision of Church and community pictures God's table and banquet which has room for all people, of all nations, of all ages. God's respect, God's embrace and God's life includes everyone. Human beings create the strategies which give pride of place to a chosen few at the Table and place the rest underneath the table to eat the scraps that fall off, or are thrown at them. In Jesus, God calls us to end divisive strategies so that all may sit and eat together at the Table for all.

Through the three articles in this book:
- the story of my pilgrimage of faith;
- my address to the Methodist Conference on 24th June 2000, and
- the sermon I delivered to the Conference on 25th June 2000.

I endeavour to share with you my theology and my challenges for church and nation for the present age.

Inderjit S. Bhogal

Pilgrimage of Faith

I am a disciple of Jesus Christ, with roots in Sikhism. I was born into a deeply religious Sikh family and grew up in an area of Kenya where people of such various faiths as Christianity, Hinduism, Sikhism and Islam lived side by side. Our house was not far away from the Sikh temple, and members of my own family shared in the leading of worship. My grandfather actively participated in the temple worship, and so did my mother, as she does to this day. I spent hours in the temple for worship, that is centred on the word of God, and where the mixture of the reading of the Scriptures and the smell of incense combine in such a way that, when you are there, the very atmosphere is like the breath of God. And serving at the table, to share in SEVA (service), during the communal meals, was part of my daily pattern of life.

The temple compound was my playground also. The resident priest, an old saintly man with flowing white beard, spent much of his time in our house. It was his home. I attended the Sikh boys and girls' school where I learned Punjabi and studied the Sikh Scriptures. In the Sikh context, my own experience of God developed into a relationship of love and trust. And all this without ever having encountered Christ, or the church. Within Sikhism I grew to understand God as Father and Mother, Friend and Companion.

After Kenya gained independence from Britain my family left in 1964. We had British passports, so we arranged to come to Britain, after spending nine months in Tanzania as refugees on coffee farms. My father found employment and accommodation for us in Dudley, near Birmingham, and I was registered at the Bluecoat Church of England school, which happened to be the nearest school to us. And for the first time in my life I experienced hostility and ridicule from my classmates because of the colour of my skin, something I had not known in Kenya.

I was the only person wearing a turban in the whole of the town in those days, and it was regularly knocked off my head. Once boys even tied me up with it. Within a month or so of our arrival in Dudley, I started attending a midweek Bible class at Vicar Street Methodist Church. There was no Sikh temple nearby. It was a meeting attended by other Sikh boys and the warmth and the friendship there were truly welcoming. I was glad to be in the centre of worship again. The knowledge that God was honoured in this place made me feel at home. The friendship was welcoming, in contrast to the hostility I experienced in school.

My first contribution to church life was to tidy the garden. I joined the members of the Bible Class on summer holidays, on pilgrimage in Scotland, climbing mountains. I listened to people talking about Christ in the meetings. I joined in prayers and in the worship. I became an avid reader of the New Testament, and became captivated - I can't think of a better word - by Christ, who is at the centre of it, and his teaching, his identification with those on the margins of society, and the story of his crucifixion. I began to share my reflections about Christ in the Bible class.

I remember kneeling down during a prayer meeting in Glasgow while we were on holiday, and making my commitment to serve in the church. There followed a time when I was confused and frightened by all that was happening to me spiritually. Why was I getting so deeply involved in the church? By this time I was attending a Sikh temple in nearby Smethwick also. Should I now just attend the temple? Why had I made this personal decision to become a disciple of Christ?

My own family was concerned and questioned my developing commitment. 'Why have you become a Christian?' they asked. 'You do not need to be a Christian to know God. You know that. God is with us and within us all. Our relationship with God is not inferior to that of Christians'. I shared those sentiments. All this caused me great pain. Why, then, if I did know God as a Sikh did I have to go and make my commitment to Christ? This was an experience that did not warm my heart. Then one day I happened to be sitting in the garden, reading the New Testament. I came to John 15:16. The words there give me strength to this very day: 'You did not choose me, I chose you'.

It is one thing to trust and to love God. It is quite another thing to know that God loves you, that God trusts you, that God calls you, that God chooses you, that God is for you on your side. I began to see the decision I had made as actually a response to God. This is the Gospel, is it not? This is the Good News, is it not? Not that we choose God, but that God chooses us. It is in this Good News that God comes to us and chooses us that my response, my strength and my vision lie. This discovery and its challenge to me was truly inspiring. My special moment was when I realised that God had chosen me, even me. My life was now centred on Jesus Christ. I found affirmation and encouragement in the story of Sadhu Sundar Singh, a Sikh who was baptised a Christian, who preached the Gospel, often being persecuted for his faith, but who retained his Sikh identity.

I told many people about my experience, about my discovery. I started to attend Sunday worship. It took a long time to venture into the church, but eventually I became a member, which caused serious alarm in our household. My brothers, who came to the Church Fellowship with me, stopped coming. My sister, who was helping in the Sunday school, stopped - in protest, I am sure, at what the church had done to me. Then the Methodist Church gave me a 'note' to preach, and in time I became ordained as a Methodist minister.

Discipleship has led me to encourage all peoples to see themselves as made in the image of God. Whatever our nationality, whatever the colour of our skin, all of us are made in the image of God. That has to be the motivation of our mission: to treat each other like that, and to make sure that everybody treats each other as the people of God. In my development as a disciple of Christ, far from abandoning my past or my Sikh culture, I have actually learned to affirm it and be proud of it. In fact, my understanding of Sikhism has grown as a result of my Christian Discipleship and I am a keen, though critical, student of Sikhism. I have seen a continuity between my upbringing as a Sikh and my Christian discipleship as important.

Jesus' first disciples followed him as Jews all their lives. Paul, after his Damascus road experience, did not cease to be a Hebrew but remained proud of his culture, although he questioned some parts of it. So I try to follow Christ within the Sikh culture. I do not describe myself as a former Sikh. Culturally I remain a Sikh. I am able to worship God and share in the communal meals with my family and others in the Sikh temples. And I wear the bracelet, the KARA, for this in Sikhism is the symbol of God's truth and justice. I wear it as a sign of my respect for Sikhs, and my family, and also to remind me that my hands must always seek the truth and justice and mercy of God.

In this search for truth and justice within my ministry I have known the greatest satisfaction, and also the greatest struggle, from sharing in the day-to-day life, witness and worship of local congregations. I enjoy the pastoral ministry, the development of worship and the building of relationships with wider neighbouring communities. I am thoroughly committed to the achievement of racial justice in the church and in society in general. Racism is a scandalous blight in our society and must be brought to an end; it operates most clearly in immigration and asylum matters and causes enormous suffering to black people.

Linked to this is the search for religious freedom. Britain, and the world, for that matter, is irreversibly multi-cultural and multi-religious. I believe that this is part of God's will and purpose, and I believe that Christians, like our Lord, must relate to different religions with respect and with a willingness to learn from them. The search for justice goes on, too, among the homeless. Churches have much to share in terms of space and resources, and should join the campaign with other agencies to provide adequate and affordable homes for everyone. The concerns for peace and reconciliation in Northern Ireland have been important throughout my experience of ministry, and I have supported and shared in the work of the Corrymeela community.

It is important for all of us to take our responsibilities seriously in these areas. We need to take time to understand the complex issues involved, to talk and exchange ideas, to implement new initiatives.

An earlier version of this article was published in 'A Continuing Faith: The 2000 Methodist Companion, Methodist Publishing House', Sept. 1999, ISBN 1 85852 386, Copyright: Trustees for Methodist Church Purposes.

A Table For All

A TABLE FOR ALL

Picture this:

I am standing in my local park in Pitsmoor, Sheffield. A multi-cultural festival is taking place. Next to me a young man is displaying posters. I read one with the words and dream of Martin Luther King.

"I have a dream that my four children one day will live in a nation where they will not be judged by the colour of their skin, but by the content of their character" [1.]

I read these words, and then I see around me the dream fulfilled in reality - an amazing gathering of black people, white people, brown people - people of all the skin colours possible: my neighbours, gathered for celebration; displaying materials, demonstrating skills and gifts. I hear the music. I watch the Bangra dancers. I smell the food, from different cultures - even my favourites: matar paneer and naan, and rasmalai were being served. People of all ages: elders sitting on the grass and benches. Young people. Women. Children queuing for ice cream. Local Christians, Sikhs, Muslims, Hindus; people of Yemeni, Somali, Pakistani, Indian, Chilean, Chinese, Irish and British origins. Among them are many who came to Britain as Refugees. They are serving each other, showing off with pride to each other. There's a spirit of respect, an atmosphere that embraces everyone. Here is vibrant life. A vision of the multi-cultural Britain of today and the future. It is possible.

My vision of Church and community pictures God's table and banquet which has room for all people, of all nations, of all ages. God's respect and God's embrace desires life for everyone. Human beings create destructive strategies which give pride of place to a chosen few at the Table and place the rest underneath it to eat the scraps that fall off, or are thrown at them. In Jesus, God shows us ways to end these strategies so that all may sit and eat together at the Table for all.

What I value in Methodism

I am a Methodist because it was at a Methodist church in Vicar Street, Dudley where I was welcomed when I was a stranger in the country having arrived from Kenya. I am a Methodist because Methodists worship God who is at the centre of everything, and follow Jesus Christ. I value:

- the Methodist emphasis on Scriptural Holiness with a strong tradition of social and political holiness;
- the Methodist tradition of giving priority to the poor. We must continue to play a part in the efforts to eradicate poverty in Britain and the rest of the world;
- Methodist music and singing;
- the Methodist insistence that Christ died for all, and that all are blessed by what John Wesley called God's "prevenient grace";
- the significant contribution of Methodists to Inter-Faith dialogue throughout the world;
- the steps Methodists have taken to affirm women's and black people's ministries bearing in mind that more has to be done;
- the Methodist class system;
- the Methodist tradition of non-conformity, though I sometimes wonder whether we can call ourselves non-conformist any more;

- the Methodist focus on food, though the legendary Methodist sandwich could have more filling and be more adventurous and we could serve Asian and Caribbean cuisine.

I value the Methodist concept of **Connexion** and our own spelling of it with a cross. Connexion, that we are one, interdependent, and part of each other, nationally and internationally, focuses Methodist spirituality for me. Connexionalism should mean that we don't use the language of centres and margins, in which centre usually means London, rather than the local church. Connexionalism means that there is such a sense of belonging to each other that decisions can be made as close to local people as possible, and that oversight can be exercised corporately. This is the heart of Methodism.

These are some of the Methodist emphases that make me feel proud of Methodism and, along with them, the people called Methodists, 70 million throughout the world. A vast and rich community whose contribution and influence ecumenically and internationally cannot be underestimated. "The world is my parish" - this is what connexionalism means today. I have a vision of connexionalism which is based on deeper maturity in relationships which have respect for who we are, which can embrace us with our differences, and which can lead to a fuller life. It is a connexionalism which is expressed in the image of a Table for all.

Let me now tell you about **Sadhu Sundar Singh of India.** His story has been an inspiration to me.

Sadhu Sundar Singh had Sikh roots. He was born in 1889 and at the age of fourteen, just after his mother's death, he had a profound religious experience in which he claimed he saw Jesus who spoke to him in Hindi. As a result, he determined to follow and to serve Jesus and, at the age of sixteen, he was baptised. His life came to be centred on Jesus and, throughout his life, he remained loyal to Jesus, though still attached to his family and proud of his own roots and culture.

This is what I attempt to do. I first came across him when I saw a picture of him at Kingsmead College in Birmingham.

What held Sadhu Sundar Singh within the church is what holds me. It is **the story of Jesus Christ.**

What I find compelling in Jesus

I find Jesus compelling because:
- Jesus expresses God who is with us all.
- Jesus gives priority to people who are poor, and gives respect to people of Other Faiths.
- Jesus eats with whoever will eat with him.
- Jesus dies abandoned by friends.

Centuries before John Wesley coined the word, Jesus Christ pointed to the "Connexionality" of God's Kingdom or Common-Wealth. He broke barriers and was "in connexion" with those that others excluded. He was a friend of those who were socially and spiritually excluded. He welcomed the poor, "the unclean", "the sinners", the harlots and publicans and ate with them. He respected them, he embraced them, and so brought them to life. He respected people of other faiths, cultures and nations. He turned over the tables which exploited people financially and spiritually, and which excluded people to such an extent that even their prayers were not valued. "My house," he declared in God's name, "shall be called a house of prayer for all nations."

And, because of this, he risked his life and died a broken man.

The one who stands by those that others reject is rejected; the one who befriends the poor is denied by his best friends; the one who respects others is mocked and ridiculed by opponents; the one who desires life abundant for others is denied life and dies a cruel death; the one who speaks truth and seeks justice is executed as a blasphemer and criminal. The one in whom we see God who is with us cries out: "My God, my God, why have you forsaken me?"

This is the point at which Jesus touched me. This is the beginning of the Gospel for me. This is the unique feature about Jesus for me in a world of many faiths and many messengers of God. Jesus identifies with those who suffer to the point of being broken and death. In this Jesus shows God's way, God's truth and God's life. Jesus illustrates a holiness of connectedness, not separateness; of intimacy, not aloofness.

Indian Dalit theology describes Jesus as the one who identifies with the Dalits, the people who are broken by society and by suffering. The term Dalit comes from "Dal" which means crushed, broken. It is the name given to broken, split red lentils. It is one of the cheapest forms of food and feeds the poor. Jesus is Dalit. Jesus and the poor are "in connexion", and we are invited into the same connexion. Jesus connects through food.

The genius of Jesus was to put food, a meal, at the centre of his community. He said "whenever you meet in my name, have a meal and remember me". The Sikh Gurus too were right to insist "First we eat, then we meet."

So often Churches present Jesus as a dull man and make following

Jesus a tedious and serious business. We've taken the fun out by focusing on meeting and not on eating. Jesus spent much time eating and drinking and partying with people. Food, the Table – not Chairs – should be at the centre of our life. The Holy Eucharist should sum up what Churches represent. It should be placed in the context of the many meals Jesus shared with others. The Holy Eucharist should nurture in us ways of living that will ensure that hunger, greed and inequality, the biggest scandals of the world's community, are ended, recognising that God desires a Table for all.

Respect, Embrace, and Life

Let me now offer you three words which are integral to my vision of 'connexionality': Respect, Embrace, and Life.

First - **RESPECT**

Respect has been highlighted by young Methodists as a primary value in the life of the church. Respect is the deepest expression of love in relationships between adults, young people and children, and, especially, for older people. Respect is the pathway to maturity in relationships. Respect is required in the relationship between human beings and the environment, human beings and animals. Respect is necessary in our relationship with God. **Relationships between Christians and people of Other Faiths can deepen faith when they are built upon mutual respect. Loyalty to Jesus goes hand in hand with openness to people of Other Faiths and the searching challenges they present to Christians.**

Respect is central to all relationships in Christian theology. Christian theology asserts that all creation bears the stamp of God and that all human beings are made in the image of God. This means that creation is sacred and has to be treated with respect; that all people are sacred and blessed, of equal worth and value, made in the image of God – this should be the starting point of our identity and self-definition. **To abuse or attack creation or a person is an assault on the image of God. Violation of human rights is a violation of the image of God in persons. Stephen Lawrence's brutal killing has come to symbolise the violence that is being done by racist attitudes and behaviour to the image of God in black people, especially young black people. Racism kills.**

To say all people are made in the image of God is to affirm there is one race, the human race with all our differences: female and male of all skin colours, shapes, sizes, abilities and sexual orientations, in one human race. Our differences enlarge us and mean that we have much to offer each other. We must learn to accommodate difference. The alternative, which we reject, is so called 'ethnic cleansing' and atrocity. God did not create different races of people and does not sanction some to be superior and others to be inferior and to serve the superior ones. God did not create some people to be "masters" who sit at Tables and others to be treated like "Dogs that eat the crumbs that fall" from the Table (Matt 15:27).

There can be no support for racism or sexism or homophobia in Christian community and theology - which declares that all people are created one and equal by God. This is not about political correctness but about justice and equal treatment.

Respect - and second, **EMBRACE.**

To embrace is to take a step on from respect and takes us to greater maturity in relationships. Embrace becomes possible in relationships of mutual respect. To embrace each other is to accept each other without requiring everyone to think and speak and appear the same. But there is a process in the movement towards embrace, if

A Table For All

in the embrace the people involved are to retain their own identities. The process takes one into one's own world, and then through education, to embrace. In mature relationships people have spaces between them. As Kahlil Gibran[2] says in The Prophet, "The oak tree and the cypress grow not in each other's shadow."

There is a profound search going on for identity in individuals, groups, communities and nations throughout the world. Here too people are feeling the need to go into their own distinctive roots and identity as in Wales, Scotland, England and Ireland. Census forms for 2001 reflect this search.

It is important for groups to focus on their own agenda, share their experiences and stories, to reflect together. Women may wish to meet on their own without men; black people may wish to meet on their own without white people; young people may wish to meet on their own without the older ones. They will focus on issues related to gender, age, colour, ability, sexual orientation and so on as appropriate.

This is necessary for the formation and nurturing of identity; for mutual support, for de-education and re-education, and to be clear about who they are so that they can **more effectively** share in the building of relationships in which peoples identity is affirmed, not denied.

This has a place if its purpose is to help everyone to move towards 'connexionality' - towards participating together in the life and witness of the church. The desire is not separate development or to inflict hurt upon anyone, but to help to mend our hurts, for the benefit of the whole church in which all belong.

Such work can help people then to educate others about themselves. Women educate men, black people educate white people, disabled educate "the able", young people educate older people and so on.

We can then move on to the stage where we can embrace each other. The spirituality of "connexion", which allows space for diversity and can accommodate difference but doesn't let this cause division between people of different opinions, implies an openness to new ideas and innovative ways of doing things. Our goal is the creation of a new community of women and men, black and white - so that in the Body of Christ each member's place is affirmed, and all belong. It is possible to create safe, embracing communities. Such embrace will be alert to dangers and ensure that safeguards are in place to protect the most vulnerable from oppressive offenders. Nations, communities, congregations, families, organisations and industry can aim to be embracing, fully participative and safe. In such relationships, the opposite to excluding people in community is sharing bread, offering hospitality. To embrace is to be prepared to sit at Table together and share bread with others. It is to be prepared to be in pilgrimage and to accompany one another.

Respect, embrace - and third, **LIFE**.

Jon Sobrino has said that the priority of the Church in El Salvador is "life and clean air". It seemed to be an odd comment, but I have come to see its validity and relevance universally, the more I have witnessed the environmental threat that is imposed by pollution in all its forms. The most obvious form of pollution is violation of air. There cannot be life without air.

Jesus expressed the God of life. In Jesus' life, suffering and death, we see that God is so passionate for all to have life that God is willing to give up God's own life.

In both creation and crucifixion God's purpose is to give life, not to take it. The story is about life, life out of nothing, life out of death. Jesus called people to full life. His community saw in him the message that he desired "life abundant" (John 10:10) for all. Life abundant is the life God desires for all – wholesome life on earth, life that is not extinguished by death, life that in union with God knows no bounds or bondage.

Jesus' test for what is good is that it is life giving. "By their fruits you shall know them", he said. The fruit is life.

Human history has been characterised by killing and death, through war, persecution, torture, malnutrition and dehydration, disease, debt and unrelenting poverty; by theories of separation, sectarianism, sexism, homophobia, racism, ethnic cleansing. Much of this remains. Does Church life and Christian theology give support to that which is life denying or to that which is life giving? **The Church, with the God of Life at the centre, cannot give assent to anything or anyone that kills.**

We should commit ourselves to a future in which we pursue respect for all life, embrace in the place of separatism, and life in all its fullness. We should seek to ensure that all that denies respect, and imposes separatism, and all that stifles life is put away. Violence in all its forms is thus resisted. The God of Life is glorified. All have a place at God's Table for all. Life is enhanced for all.

Respect for who we are as people; embrace of us with our differences: this can guarantee a fuller life for all - a connexionalism expressed in the image of a Table for all. These are themes that need to be integral to our theology of "connexionalism".

We have to consider all church life, theology, evangelism, mission and ministry from this perspective. Judge them by their fruit. I would also apply this test to all national life and politics. The primary fruit is life. Where life is not enhanced for all, we should protest. To protest is to be for life.

The nation and church can be judged by how we treat people who are most vulnerable, whose life is threatened most. This is the ultimate test of any spirituality, morality and theology. The Bible repeatedly singles out "the widow, the orphan and the stranger." In our times I suggest they would be the elderly, the children and "the stranger" - someone who is different. What is the treatment of the elderly, the children and the stranger by the nation and the Churches? What, for example, is our nation's treatment of those who flee from their homes for the sake of their lives, to seek refuge and asylum here – today's strangers?

Asylum Seekers

There are 50 million uprooted people around the world. Many of them take refuge in neighbouring countries. Less than one million make their way to Europe. Less than 100,000 come to Britain.

The situation is now scandalous.

Hundreds of refugees are exploited or getting killed in horrific circumstances en route. Many of those who do arrive here are incarcerated in prisons and detention centres. Others are dispersed to poor housing away from support systems, and are allowed below poverty level vouchers for a mean existence and then bullied for begging. Not much sign of respect, embrace and life here. Some newspapers and politicians deepen the crisis by using emotive language of "bogus" and "flooding". **The abusive ways in which Asylum Seekers are treated mocks the image of God in their human being.**

If people go from torture to torture that is like going from crucifixion to crucifixion. Theologically that is not acceptable. Seeking people's welfare and fullness of life is more in keeping with God's will and purposes.

The use of prisons and detention centres to detain Asylum Seekers should be discontinued. In exceptional circumstances people should be held in warden assisted hostels. Asylum seekers should be accommodated more carefully, in habitable homes, ensuring proper care and support – in partnership with local communities. Christians have resources to assist with accommodation. Refugees and Asylum Seekers are human beings too. I admire their resourcefulness to survive. They should not be seen as a drain on the economy or a burden on the Tax Payer, but as people who can make a positive contribution. Britain, with an ageing population, will need to accommodate and employ more people from overseas in the future.

We should press Government for new Immigration and Asylum Laws and Procedures which recognise the multi-cultural identity of Britain today and are based on respect for people, embrace diversity, are life enhancing and are created in partnership – in connexion – with all other nations of the world, not just European.

I have expressed my own concerns by writing letters to the Prime Minister and to the Home Secretary asking for a fair deal for Asylum

Seekers, and by engaging in pilgrimages of prayer and fasting. I needed to protest and to express my anger at detention of Asylum Seekers. We can all do something with dignity and creativity. In Rothwell a group of women welcomed and fed me when I appeared as a stranger among them on my pilgrimage. I applaud and thank every individual, group, congregation and organisation that challenges injustices and seeks a fairer deal for Asylum Seekers.

God is outraged when "the stranger residing among you suffers extortion" (Ezek 22:7). Churches have to express and demonstrate this holy outrage.

Theology begins when we ask why is it like this? Spirituality begins with an honesty about reality.

Church Life

So how does Methodism measure up? How does the congregation you worship and serve with look from this perspective? Do **we** respect, embrace, give life to each other? Is the Table in our communities God's Table for all? Are we able to eat with each other in the name of Jesus? Are we in connexion with those who find themselves rejected by others, with those who feel broken by life's experiences, the most vulnerable? Do we reflect the Spirit of Christ who befriended the poor and ate with all who would eat with him? Where we do, others may respect and embrace Church more and wish to participate in its life; where we do not, we should not be surprised if people reject Church.

Our records reflect a declining base. This does raise questions about us. We cannot ignore these but should not go into deep depression about it. There are small congregations in urban and rural areas, fearful of the future. Just surviving is an achievement. I know congregations of predominantly older people with no one under the age of 60. With an ageing population we can expect such congregations. They need support. Enhancing the quality of life for older people includes churches welcoming and respecting them.

The predominantly younger congregation I minister with at Wincobank Chapel is based in a situation everyone seems to be abandoning. Most of the houses have now been pulled down. We have a damp and broken but beautiful little chapel, 160 years old. No drainage. No security. No heating. No collection. Little money. Holes in windows. But our spirits are not damp. Church is about being together – all ages, eating, partying, worshipping and working together and in partnership with others, and not just for one hour a week. The Church puts children first. It is Bible and prayer centred. We have found a way of being Church in a fragmented, inner city context. We are not a large congregation but we are a dynamic one. We are committed to staying, and playing our part in the regeneration and coming to life again of the Estate, arguing that regeneration is about putting people first, not profits; about putting homes and safety first, not shops. It is about helping to rebuild the community.

Recently we visited together the Amelia Trust Farm, near Cardiff, and discovered a different expression of Church in a rural context. The Farm, set in 160 acres of land, includes opportunities for new skills to be learned, and a new sense of belonging, through workshops, music, art and through working with animals, trees and soil. Through listening, supporting, encouraging and pastoral care, the Farm is a significant place for a range of individuals and groups. People experience change in lives and lifestyle. The Farm respects and embraces many who otherwise have felt rejected. For many the Farm is their Church, through which they feel able to offer their best.

We have shared in Jubilee 2000 which used an obscure and out of date idea to demonstrate what influence churches can have in the public and political arena when we work together. The campaign has caught the imagination of people outside the church too.

Church now competes with many other attractions. Many people are not familiar with Jesus' story. Church has no place in their lives. We have therefore to be creative and imaginative and develop new patterns of being church - in meaningful ways in which the experience and message of the Kingdom of God reaches out to people where they are. Always, whatever the context, rural, urban, suburban, Church and connexionalism should respect and affirm all people, embracing different identities, cultures and languages; and not stifle but give, renew and enhance life for all.

Wincobank Chapel - and there are many like it - the Farm and Jubilee 2000 inspire us to get away from being depressed about decline. People from around the world could tell many similar stories of Christians living out the gospel with little resources in different environments.

Conclusion

As Maya Angelou says: "The question is not how to survive but how to thrive with passion, compassion humour and style."

Christians have a life-giving, life-transforming story of Jesus as a special gift to share in a world of many faiths. We must tell his story well and live by it. It is a story which helps us to interpret all life. There is much in Methodist heritage we can contribute. We can build on it by developing a solid financial base and supporting relevant theological education to equip the church for a new future. We need strategies that will particularly nurture and support young people, black and white, to use their experiences and gifts.

The situation in which we now exist presents new insights and challenges which we can meet with enthusiasm, not despair. We will learn much if we listen to others with respect. God is doing new, creative things in the world and church life. Congregations are discovering new ways of being church.

I anticipate this year and the future with confidence. I invite you to do so also. Always, we shall serve the present age, our calling to fulfil.

Notes:

[1] Quoted in Kenneth Slack, *Martin Luther King*, page 85, SCM Press Ltd., London, 1970

[1] Kahil Gibran, *The Prophet*, page 19, Heinemann, London, 1976

A TABLE IN THE WILDERNESS?

The sermon preached at the Methodist Conference, Huddersfield on Sunday 25th June, 2000

Text: "A Table in the Wilderness?" Ps 78.19

Let us Pray.

> May the words of my mouth
> And the meditation of our hearts
> This morning – and throughout the week
> Reflect the Spirit of Christ
> And be acceptable to you
> Dear God
> Whose name is Truth
> Whose way is Just
> Whose desire for all is Life
> And for all to be treated as guests of honour at your table.
> Amen.

What a marvellously crazy idea: a table in the wilderness. Community celebration – a party in the wilderness. It's about as crazy as having Conference in Huddersfield.

A Table For All

It's about as mad as celebrating the holy eucharist in some of the contexts we represent. Like the Flower Estate in Sheffield where I share in ministry – a kind of waste land where houses have been knocked down, an area people are moving out of.

When the children of Israel were held captive in Egypt, Moses and Aaron went to Pharaoh and said "thus says the Lord ... Let my people go, so that they may celebrate a festival (feast) with me in the wilderness" (Ex. 5:1)

What an image: to celebrate a festival, a party with God in the wilderness. God the party-goer wants a party – a rave up in the open air. God chooses to celebrate in the wilderness, not in the place of captivity and oppression; even though the Psalmist could sing "You prepare a table for me in the presence of mine enemies, you treat me like an honoured guest". While those in power might let me feed on scraps that fall off their table, you treat me like an honoured guest.

There were of course those who questioned this. "Can God spread a Table in the wilderness? Even though he struck the rock so that the water gushed out and torrents overflowed, can he also give bread ..." (Ps 78.19).

Will there be food at the party? Can God spread a table in the wilderness?

Was this also the inward prayer of Elijah who fled "a days journey into the wilderness" and sat under a tree with an abject sense of failure, fearing for his life, feeling suicidal, wishing to die ... when an angel came to him with bread and said "Get up and eat"?

Whatever else you do, when you are not well, don't stop eating.

And did all these images look back to Abraham sharing a meal with "angels" in the wilderness, under the oaks of Mamre? Can we also anticipate in these meals Jesus eating food with multitudes in the countryside, in their homes, or on the beach?

There is a tradition in scripture of God providing manna, bread in the wilderness. The answer to the psalmist's rhetorical question would be clear to all the hearers: Yes. God can prepare a table in the wilderness, and a table in the midst of "enemies" even, and treat people as honoured guests without laying any conditions except this: have enough for your need, don't be overcome with greed which leads to unfairness and waste.

Have a party. But don't be greedy.

A table in the wilderness...
That people may celebrate with me in the wilderness ....

IN THE WILDERNESS!
In the place that people are inclined to steer clear of, to avoid.
In the place where life is risky.
In the place which can threaten to destroy life.
In the place which can be beautiful but remote, arid and leave one exposed, vulnerable.
In the place which can be vast, where one can get lost, and in which one may expect to be for a long time.
The Bible describes a desert as a wilderness and sees it in positive terms too:

- it is the place of encounter with God;
- it is the place where God's word is heard;
- it is where temptation is wrestled with;
- it is where God provides for people the miracle of water and food for each day;
- it is where prophets too find refuge and are ministered to by angels;
- it is where community with all its pitfalls is forged.

IN THE WILDERNESS

Can God provide "a table in the wilderness"?

Yes, God can prepare a table even in a place of oppression and in the presence of "enemies" and treat you like an honoured guest. But he will only prepare a table in order to **celebrate** where there is freedom from oppression, even if that means providing a table in the wilderness. There can be no party when there is oppression.

Where is the wilderness for us, for you, for the church in which you worship and serve?

What is the place you dread?

The place you avoid?

The place you would choose not to visit or live in?

Is it that dull, monotonous, boring relationship which you find oppressive and which is exhausting?

Is it the place of work in which you feel unfulfilled, or a new direction you are being pushed into?

Is it the experience of unemployment?

Is it the neighbourhood in which your church is set?

A Table For All

Is it your congregation in which you feel isolated?

God wants to celebrate a feast with you there.

This all sounds fun here in Huddersfield, in these surroundings.

God at least gives honour and worth to you, and longs to celebrate a feast with you there.

But:
Can God prepare a table for those who have no home and no table?
Can God prepare a table for the people in places of famine?
Can God prepare a table for asylum seekers living in poverty and who have to beg in a hostile environment?

I decided to reflect on this by sitting where homeless people sit in Sheffield.

> *Graham is homeless. He says people call him a "tramp" and sometimes give him money. He lives on the streets of Sheffield where I have got to know him well. As a walker, he gave me sound advice as I prepared to walk along roads from Sheffield to London. I saw him recently, he was sitting on a concrete bench in the city centre. He had a bandage round his head and one around a foot. "Banged into a wall" he said.*

> *As we got into conversation I asked him to help me. I'm working on a sermon about tables and bread and parties in the wilderness, I said. It seems a bit odd, but can you help me?*

A Table For All

"I love bread" he said.

He reached into a carrier bag beside him. His boots and walking stick were by the bag. Out of the bag he fetched bread.

"I always have bread" he said. "I know a shop. I turn up just before closing time. They give me a couple of loaves. With it I feed myself and my brothers and sisters who are poor" He talked to me about all those homeless ones who walk at night as others sleep.

He held out a large round cob.

"This is made from rye. I love it – my favourite." He said, "try some."

He broke off a large piece with his rugged hands and held it out to me. I received it and said "Amen" and ate it in bits over several minutes.

As I ate it, he unpacked his carrier bag and brought out different kinds of bread and placed it all on the concrete slab bench which had now become a table. Suddenly I was having a meal, and he was the host. Each loaf was held up and its contents were described. I was given a piece from each loaf.

"You need good red wine with this bread ... it would be a good one for your communion at church".

"You need to eat this bread with cheese ..."

A Table For All

All around us a city centre environment with its own beauty, but a wilderness with a lifestyle of grabbing and greed and of profit before people. People racing about. Some sitting down to rest. Before me now a parable of the text: "a table in the wilderness."

I was being fed by one of the poorest people I know. I was a guest of honour at a table in the wilderness. "You treat me like an honoured guest."

After this feast I went and sat in a fast food bar for a while. What a contrast. The one described as a "tramp" described himself as a "connoisseur of bread". We sat and talked for an hour. In the fast food restaurant people came and ate bland food made tasty by additives. They sat for 10-15 minutes to eat and went. They showed no respect for food, no respect for bread. They were not treated as honoured guests. They had no capacity to sit, to taste, to talk. No wonder that, before Jesus fed a multitude with bread, he said "Make the people sit down".

The table is set/spread in the wilderness, in the midst of all that threatens.

- Greed
- Decline
- Loneliness
- Homelessness
- Poverty
- How asylum seekers are treated

A Table For All

- Church on broken down housing estate
- Church in agricultural poverty
- Globalism
- Capitalism and socialism
- Selfishness
- Individualism
- Get out of it what you can culture
- ½m tonnes of food thrown away in UK each year

We have to learn to celebrate and feast with God in our wilderness.

The table is an important symbol in a culture dominated by chairs. Jesus sets a table in the midst of his community.

The eucharistic table –

Is it the church's table which is so often an excluding one, or is it Jesus's table which is an including one?

Which is the table that Jesus turns over?
  - the table that exploits, the table that excludes?
  - the table that exists on "trickle down" theory at which some eat the scraps that fall off?
  - the unfair table which allows hunger?

Can the Lord prepare a table in the wilderness?

Yes. The Lord welcomes and treats all as "honoured guests" as in Psalm 23. The Lord welcomes children and even those who betray him. In the midst of all the shit celebrate eating with each other, drink wine, enjoy time with your lover, wear good clothes (Eccl 9:7-9), build relationships, care for and provide for each other, end hunger so that no one has to eat the scraps that fall off tables.

The Lord's table is prepared in the midst of contexts and realities that threaten life, in contexts we may prefer to avoid.

It challenges greed and seeks an end to hunger in a world of plenty.

It challenges the scandal of church disunity.

It calls for an end to economic structures that create hunger and famine.

God prepares a banquet in the wilderness, a celebration in the midst of all that threatens. It is in the wilderness that God teaches much, woos people, calls, affirms, tests, feeds. Like the poor "tramp", God feeds us out of God's bounty and treats us all with honour. A foretaste of the heavenly banquet prepared for all.